Our
Scarlet Blue
Wounds

Emmett Wheatfall

Our Scarlet Blue Wounds
©2019 by Emmett Wheatfall

http://emmettwheatfall.com

Fernwood Press
Newberg, Oregon
www.fernwoodpress.com

Cover image: Shalom Mwenesi
Cover design: Mareesa Fawver Moss

Printed in the United States of America

ISBN 978-1-59498-064-0

If James Baldwin was a god (idol)
Ta-Nehisi Coates is your prophet

To the Negro
Emmett Wheatfall

I dedicate this book to the brilliant black intellectual

Ta-Nehisi Coates

Contents

Poetry is the only utterly free space for language
that I'm aware of,
and that is what makes it indispensable to me,
and also what makes writing it and reading it a political act.

Kathleen Ossip
June 1, 2017

Kathleen Ossip is the author of three books of poems,
including *The Do-Over*,
a New York Times Editors' Choice.

Foreword

As I write this, a wall is being built around the southern lip of our country; hate groups are being reclassified by the top echelon of our government as "patriots"; so far, two deadly mass shootings have occurred each month in 2019; and youth firearm fatalities, predominantly people of color, have reached "epidemic proportions." To quote Dr. Charles Hennekens, the senior author of a massive study by Florida Atlantic University's Schmidt College of Medicine:

> It is sobering that in 2017, there were 144 police officers who died in the line of duty and about 1,000 active duty military throughout the world who died, whereas 2,462 school-age children were killed by firearms.

Yet, as blossoms struggling up through the cracks in pavement, there are seeds of hope. Confederate statues are toppling. Streets in many major cities are being renamed for civil rights heroes. Forty-four percent of Americans, a majority of the study, claim Barack Obama was the best president of their lifetime. Youth are hitting the streets in droves to protest inequality and demand action from officials. Working class communities are banding together to fight hate. And poets from outside the predominantly white university establishment are finally being heard—and celebrated.

It's into this maelstrom of cultural divisiveness that prolific poet Emmett Wheatfall's latest collection, *Our Scarlet Blue Wounds*, enters the world. As both a call to witness and a plea for action, Wheatfall's poems are absolutely necessary. This is the kind of book that reminds you, urgently, ungently, that an active citizenry is required of a working democracy. I became a better citizen after living for a time in Wheatfall's world, which is our world with the lights turned on: luminous, ugly, true. In "Constitution," he places this burden to witness directly, heavily, on our communal shoulders:

> By you and on me is penned
> America's liberty

Whitmanesque in scale, and as timeless, heartbreaking, desperately hopeful, the poem "O, America!" takes us by the shirt collar and lifts us up so we can look the poet squarely in the eye:

> What wrath is there
> at these bountiful shores, these
> borderless borders

Here, there are no distinctions between you and me,

between one and another nation; our responsibilities, and the opportunities that rise mightily from them, are essential elements of our being: the darkness and light, the critical and celebratory, the abstract and corporeal. In the end, everything is of the body, affects the body, hurts and heals and hurts again a real body with a heart and lungs and family and fears and loves and a name others may try to erase for their own culturally nefarious purposes. I'm reminded in Wheatfall's vision of George Oppen's epic "Of Being Numerous," which begins:

> There are things
> We live among 'and to see them
> Is to know ourselves'.
>
> Occurrence, a part
> Of an infinite series,
>
> The sad marvels;
>
> Of this was told
> A tale of our wickedness.
> It is not our wickedness.

Sad marvels, indeed. Wickedness. Witness. History as an "infinite series" of wrongdoings, then struggles to right this great ship we're all on. In amalgamating the politically direct and emotionally nuanced, I'm seeing something in Wheatfall's poetry that's entirely (and unfortunately) familiar, cast through a uniquely authentic lens. He's created new ways for me to wrestle with my own privilege and legacy, those small and often unrecognized ways I affect and am affected by my neighbors and country. His poems "bring to bear our bruises" ["A Patriot's Poem"]. They redefine patriotism. Ideologically aware, they wield relentless optimism and raw imagination as weapons against apathy.

But where does he find this optimism? How does he find meaning, in the Viktor Frankl sense, when faced with white nationalism and crumbling public schools and victim blaming and historical traumas and the daily murder of black men and women right outside our windows? For an answer, I look to Langston Hughes' inimitable lines [from "Dreams"]:

> Hold fast to dreams
> For if dreams die
> Life is a broken-winged bird
> That cannot fly.

Wheatfall shares Hughes' bold, open-hearted, spiritual, and assertively honest vision. He shows us how the roots of love grow deep in the soil of sacrifice. He illustrates the intensely complex relationship between idealism and realism. His poems hurt in just the right way. And it's no small feat opening one's own racial and cultural wounds for the world to see. It takes courage. It takes trust that a country will recognize itself, and its complicity, in those wounds. And Wheatfall trusts us to witness along with him. He proves himself ready and willing, even eager, to, as the titular poem in this collection demands, "build a new world" together.

—John Sibley Williams

Our Scarlet Blue Wounds

On the heels of something great, I'll take you there.
Consider failure the cause célèbre it is. Let's build a new world.
Out of clay, let us hew a stone absent despair,
      from 55-year-old timber, let us whittle a new age.

      Let love love whomever it loves.

A resolution proffered by the bourgeois isn't necessary.
We will secretly build new cities near rivers and deep within valleys,
And in the times of fire and flood we will lift like eagles to aeries.
Let us bleed red blood everywhere bearing our scarlet blue wounds.

      Let love love whomever it loves.

Should we mark every soul with a magic marker—yes!—
doing so before we return to the dust that's prepared for us?
May we, the old, die young, and you, the young, live forever.
      Might we agree to return here again?

Let love love whomever it loves.

Constitution

I am written because I will not hurt anyone, and
neither should you.
"What do you mean?" said pen to paper. "How far is
fantasy from reality?"
"The truth I hold is self-evident," said paper. "What
truth?" replied the pen.
"We the People..." Let us therefore challenge the living
and laud reverence
for the dead. "By you and on me is penned America's
liberty," said paper.

Democracy Is Not Working

Democracy is not working.

Shackled at ankles are life, liberty,
and the pursuit of happiness.

Democracy is not working.

America's oligarchs are lofty larks
lording now and for generations to come.

Democracy is not working.

Charter schools chafe away at public
schools that once ruled education.

Democracy is not working.

Blackface is again the new and old face, as
orange is the new black.

Democracy is not working.

White nationalism, the Klan, white
supremacy and neo-Nazism mark your
land and my land,

"From California to the New York
Island / From the Redwood Forest to the
gulf stream waters /..."

Democracy is not working.

America's Noble Ideals

A madman has arisen
With a mad face
Using mean words
That rally racists
In a nation bewildered
By wantonness
From wanton men
And wanton women
Who weary
The huddled masses
In the midst of
America's noble ideals

O, America!

O, America!
O, sweet America.
How sour are your grapes?
    What wrath is there
    on this the threshold that is liberty,
    this red, white, and blue carpet,
    stained blood red,
    white with truth self-evident,
    bruises borne blue on bodies of
    old and young,
    people of color, slave and free, the
    innocent unjustly burdened?

O, America!
O, sweet America.
How sour are your grapes?
    What wrath is there
    at these bountiful shores, these
    borderless borders; and yes,
    they who are tired, poor, these huddled
    masses? Where is the lamp-light that
    once lighted this our path
    to and from the halls of
    truth, justice, and the American ideal?
    What is this wrath?

O, America!

O, sweet America.

How sour are your grapes?

    What wrath is there

    that an ill-tempered man with his

    quiver full of executive orders, exacting

    privilege, rogue arrogance

    with impunity of soul, governing each day?

    Why are you not mourning?

    Why is your soul not discontent?

    Lift up your head again and make

    low agin' him, that belligerent beast.

O, America!

O, sweet America.

How sour are your grapes?

    What wrath is there

    regarding your neighbor's missing children,

    separation of husband and wife,

    of families, the poorest cities,

    farming and rural America?

    What of the marginalized and the

    disenfranchised?

O, America!

    O, sweet America.

How sour are your grapes?

How sour are your grapes?

    O, sweet America.

'Tis of thee, I ask.

Confirmation Hearing

Of potential
is pulp, paper's predecessor,
post canvas for literature, fiction,

poetics.

She just grabbed my ass!

A wife can do that; just grab
her husband's ass. My ass? It's hers.
She's got paper, post pulp,

signed,
sealed.

At this time
I'm writing poetry. At least I believe
I am.

It's prose poetry.

U.S. Representative John Lewis just said,
"We all live in the same house."

He speaks not of White House
built by slaves. No, no, he speaks of
constitution—U.S. Constitution,

made of paper,
subsequent to pulp,
then to canvas for literature, fiction,

poetics.

Eagle

Perhaps?

The Eagle will take flight
after fortnight comes,
whose image, obscures in visible
moonlight.

Ground to pulp is truth to fiction.
Skepticism supersedes powers
of patriotic conviction when liberty
ends.

Battles rage like fruitless utility
as the populous watch and wait with
futility. Will Eagle return to
perch?

Perhaps?

Upon My Soul

Without liberty
    there can be no license.
        Think apartheid.
Tragically for the caged bird
    absent is Constitution.
        Words frame,
bars confine.
    Upon my soul I bear
        clipped wings.
From my cage
    I often see the rise of morning
        and setting of evening.
Unable to argue with my captor
    I make strange noises,
        bang on my cage,
crap on newspapered floor.
    I listen as constitutional
        scholars argue
the merits of originalism
    versus interpretivism,
        repeating back to my captor
article after article
    of Constitution.
        There comes no freedom.

If only I could be Steve Biko.
What's coming to me
is a Steve Biko death.
Given will be my creative protest.
This bird cries, "Freedom!
Freedom!"

Refresh the Tree of Liberty

Fools follow tyrants.

    Sit down to a beer with wrath, then
crush sour grapes.

    Turn deception into typical vitriol.
Present facts for-certain alternatives.

    Catch the tyrant's whiff, then
exhale where it's going.

    There should be—a whiff that is.
From all winsome tyrants flee.

    If they do advance lies for fake news,
refresh liberty's tree with truth—or,

    blood will do.

Give Me Death

Who is he or she
Or the gender-neutral pronoun
That takes a life

Who snuffs out
The light in a single individual's eyes
Or that of a nation

How can you love
A musket-ball more than
Life in shadows

A Patriot's Poem

Darkness is deep down here
Our dayward egress upward—steep
We kneel before our native flag
O' glory Stars and Stripes
Bring to light our scarlet bruises
O' glory Stars and Stripes
Bring to bear our bruises blue

They Will Not Prevail

When is it ever enough for racists racing up
hillsides, marching militaristically in city streets
and country roads, populating city parks and town
squares, waving

wildly Nazi and racist symbols from WWII's
vanquished foes; shouting prescribed rhetoric of
fascists, singing the lyrics of supremacy, declaring and
advocating the ilk of their evil? They will not prevail.

When is it ever enough for religious zealots hiding
behind masks, militaristically marshaling against
the innocent, murdering and massacring under
the guise

of righteousness, advancing a theology tempered
in a teapot where its tea is the porridge of poison?
It being the brisk brew of evil. These people
are deceived. They will not prevail.

When is it ever enough for the privileged, whether
by race, class, economics, politics; be it titled
residency, domain or dominion; knowledge, or
the feigning of

ignorance; of lineage, or ill-gotten gain;
advancing aggression and micro-aggressions
against the poor, marginalized, the so-called
"Other"? Be it understood, they will not prevail.

Love Is Freedom (Liu Xiaobo)

> The lovers even China couldn't keep apart
> The enduring love story of Nobel Peace Prize laureate
> Liu Xiaobo and Liu Xia.
>
> —CNN

When a photograph,
absent a thousand words, summons,
lays hold to places under duress;
and my imagination suggests I pause—
it's noteworthy.

Nobel Peace Prize Laureate
Liu Xiaobo and Liu Xia in embrace,
posed for a snapshot photograph that
documents and authenticates
their love, their fidelity.

Love is freedom unabridged.
Love never dies. Love lives long after
hummingbirds take to flight,
when they have slipped their wiry cage.

Love is not Chinese. Love is not
machinations of East nor West.
Love is freedom. Like a hummingbird,
Liu Xiaobo has taken to flight; he's a
hummingbird having slipped his wiry cage.

Long last love Liu Xia.
Listen to what the hummingbird sings.
Liu Xiaobo is free now. One day
you too will take to flight, slip the
wiry cage, for love is freedom.

The Black Body

An artistic form of black beauty is to paint
the body of black men and women. Let the
artist go about glorifying the black body,
whether on canvas or without. Why? In our
America, with such impunity the black body
continues to be destroyed. The intellectual
Ta-Nehisi Coates, our James Baldwin, states,

"In America, it is traditional to destroy the
black body—it is heritage."

Therefore, let black men and women, artists
who paint black men and women, be given to
sanctifying blackness—for the beauty of the
black body is black strength; lest forgotten are
our scarlet blue wounds.

Nation of Thieves

Who thinks cessation while living
None in this generation
For we are a nation of thieves
Flush with the boldness of boll weevils
Sealing our fate with vanity
Polished pots bearing no reflection
The last shall come to an end
Where grace is a disgrace
The faint heart will not beat strongly
Temporal the timing of tulips
Without complaint fate submits
Who thinks cessation while living

At the Edge of America

So, you want to tell us your story.
How can we hear you without our children?
Where are our babies?
We ask you because our babies cannot
ask where we are.
We are here, at the edge of America,
where we are told, "Give me your tired, your poor,
your huddled masses." No! We are
asking you,

> Where are our babies?
> Where are our children? Of our babies
> we need to give them suck, we need to
> swaddle them, we need to fill their faces
> with kisses, and let them hear us speak
> not in yours, but our native tongue.

So, you want to tell us your national story.
We don't want to hear how your ancestors
came to the edge of America by way
of the sea. We care not that you
threw tea into the Boston Harbor; we
care not how one of your kind sewed stars
and stripes; we care not how you declared
independence from England, formed
an imperfect union of 50 states, and now
call yourselves the United States.

We are here, at the edge of America,
where we are told, "Give me your tired, your poor,
your huddled masses." No! We are
asking you,

> Where are our babies?
> Where are our children? Of our babies
> we need to give them suck, we need to
> swaddle them, we need to fill their faces
> with kisses, and let them hear us speak
> not in yours, but our native tongue.

Common Humanity

Adam, alongside Eve,
has journeyed among the stars,
having been to the moon and back,
placed two rovers on unmarred
surfaces of the red planet
called Mars;

    as well as,

sanctioned living space
in a space station. From there looked
back and beheld what God sees and
the moon knows, as those same stars
still summon the return of both
Adam and Eve

    into common humanity.

Boxed-In

I saw a man with no teeth,
he smiled at me.

I bumped into a woman who had no feet,
she crawled to me.

I hugged a child with no arms, we
laughed until I cried.

A blind man called to me. Why
couldn't I see where he was calling from?

A homeless man cursed at me,
afterward, he and I shared his beer.

A streetwalker propositioned me,
I replied, "Thank you, but no thank you,"

then named that street after her.

Some Americans are boxed-in.
Some people are like me.

Some are like them.

Go Back to Mexico!

"Go back to Mexico!" shouts an elderly woman.
This elderly white woman felt emboldened.
much the way a street protester shouts when
offering ardent dissent at a political rally.

Astonished is the Latin American cashier. Diego
is not from Mexico. Diego is from Maryland. He
immigrated to the United States with his father,
his mother, two siblings, two uncles and an aunt.

Aisle 6 is where the chili pepper is kept. A tall
and stout Texan is offering sushi samples. The
Texan asks the elderly woman, "Would you like to
try one?" She says, "Why yes," with a sultry smile.

Second-Class Citizen

What do you know about self-determination?
Israelis do. Palestinians do. Black South Africans did.
The Negro does. In other regards others still do;
slowly, as if drip-drying faucets, as Native peoples
have all but been disappeared.

And there you are mining your way through this
your begotten life, equipped with the potential of
intellect and a set of bare hands that owe a debt of
gratitude to black slaves who precede you.

What do you know about self-determination?
Quakers do. Mennonites do. The Bracero worker did.
The immigrant does. In other regards others still do;
undocumented and living in fear of the all-powerful
Immigration and Customs Enforcement agent.

And then there's you. Hop, skipping and jumping
your way through life. Leaping over less-fortunate
peoples. Skipping due to invisible affirmative action.
Jumping via the platform and trampoline of privilege.

What do you know about self-determination?
Rich men do. Poor women do. The oligarch, he did.
The tyrannical does. In other regards others still do;
with gentle sleight of hand the marginalized dismissed
and "others" sanctioned to poverty, even death.

And then there is me, a second-class citizen in
the nation of my birth. Imagine how sad it is
to be seated at the table only to realize you're not
really present in the grand scheme of dreaming.

What do you know about self-determination?
The dead don't. Actuaries don't. Jesus Christ, he did.
A believer does. In other regards others still do;
at the center of self-determination and not narcissism,
but with an ever-abiding sense of self-worth.

Unconscious Bias

When a white man
Wearing a white wig
Clothed in a black robe
Sits in judgment
Of a black woman
Wearing a black wig
And clothed in a
Striped white jumpsuit—
It should signal
An injustice
Perpetrated by
An unconscious bias

The Veteran with No Legs

I saw a veteran with no legs wearing a pair of pants.
I offered that woman my respect; the kind with honor.
It felt so right on that cold day to give her my jacket,
the one with the NIKE swoosh emblemized on its back.
Colin Kaepernick came to mind. I then knelt beside her.
Given I had no hands, she laid upon me the Stars and
Stripes, just in case other Veterans of Foreign Wars joined us.

Shame on this City

My views are not without foundation.

For between my teeth sprout daffodils.
I always sidestep makeshift homes
where the downtrodden sit or lay. As do
bypassing plebs and business owners.

KGW-TV has yet to ask my opinion.
It wouldn't behoove KGW to do so.
My commentary about fake news is
in play because I know everything.
Obviously, KGW doesn't know that.

Spinning on its axis the earth listens to
Otis Redding singing (sittin' on) The Dock
Of The Bay. Because a tsunami has yet to
advance beyond some imaginary red line
established by NOAA. Hey! I'm startled.

A doomed man froze to death yesterday
in the doorway of a business. He had not fallen,
but went to sleep covered only by
a blanket, graced only by a pillow beneath
his head. Shame on this city.

It wasn't time to play hardball with
the homeless. Hardball? Pun? Certainly
unintended. I should have done something.
Honestly, I knew not what to do. Honestly,
I knew he was homeless, cold, wet, given his

scarlet blue wounds in the vestibule.
Between my teeth sprout daffodils.
I will never again sidestep makeshift homes
where the downtrodden sit or lay. Maybe the
bypassing plebs and business owners still do.

My views are not without foundation.

Intersectionality

You see that girl with a girl.
I see her, too.
You are in love with her.
I am, too.
Would it make a difference
if she knew you and I
are in love with her;
you being cisgender male
and I, cisgender female?

When did love
capture our attention,
hold at bay our intentions
and inhibitions?

You see that girl with a girl.
I see her, too.
Where from does phobia come?
Ungoverned by logic is this
intersection.

You see that girl with a girl.
I see her, too.
We are in love at the crossroad
of sexuality.

Why does this world hate them?
Why must it hurt us?
At the intersection of our
sexuality we bear bruises,
our scarlet blue wounds.

Crackers

Who's
eaten unleavened bread,
despised white cheddar,
a hand full of
25 crackers
being white?

I've met some
half-baked crackers before.

They were some
unleavened looking crackers
too.
So much so,
I couldn't sip
my vanilla milkshake.

I Read Wallace Stevens Poem...

...Like Decorations in a Nigger Cemetery.
Oh! I meant to say, the revered Wallace Stevens;
him being that noted poet of yesteryears.

If I were to have a word with the late great
Wallace Stevens, would I decorate; no, desecrate
his cemetery with *Like Decorations*???

Nigger is a referenced name, it's not
a name I answer to. The tulips and petunias,
lilacs and daffodils that will grace my grave;

the tombstone that will not tumble
given a terrible tempest of wind where again
In the far South the sun of autumn is passing.

To the Negro

Do not seek refuge in your past
The door to reentry is closed

"We Shall Overcome" is a common's
Unanswerable as expanding universe

Pursuit of an answer for "Why"
Consider the blackness of celestial tapestry

Curse trees for their branches if necessary
Forget not the horror of a French guillotine

That gift by the French to America
It was meant for you, too

America's flag waves red, white, and blue
In black ink, liberty's been codified

Despite being hung high
Sweet chariots always swung low

"Say it loud, I'm black, and I'm proud!"
Tweet it, Facebook it, Instagram it

Notice the Trump in the fold of hands
It's a card you've seen played before

#BlackLivesMatter isn't only a mantra
Beware of ever-present antimatter

Silver haired poets the epitome?

Your silence is equivalent to consent

If James Baldwin was a god (idol)
Ta-Nehisi Coates is your prophet

Your currency is green
For God's sake trust in God

A poem does not require rhyme
It should contain a sense of reason

Have you all but given up?
Harriet Tubman said, "Keep going!"

Attar said, "Here comes a sea /
Followed by an ocean"

No matter the wish, you must be
Prepared for consequence

The Un-Blurring of the Brown Skin Man:
A Poem by a Citizen Poet

To be blown up is not to be blown up

What does the Constitution say
Did expediency trump this nation's laws
Up in smoke body parts and blood
Where was due process

What does the Constitution say

Burst upon this man an ultra–white flash
Who can for cause bear scarlet blue wounds
The un–blurring of the brown skin man
How far has the flag frayed

Did expediency trump this nation's laws

What happened to apprehension
Whereupon what sword has righteousness fallen
Why has improvised destruction come
Is the device now the devise

Up in smoke body parts and blood

Once there was the hangman's noose
Then came the electric chair
Promulgated the sniper's bullet
Now the advent of C–4 (explosive)

Where was due process

Right to legal representation
Right to public trial
Right to trial by jury
Summary judgment by execution???

The United States
A nation of laws
Is it not
Is it not
Is it not

Asks the citizen poet

How Easily the White Professor Forgets

> The United States is an immigrant country.
> How we easily forget our own heritage.
>
> —Anonymous
> A Christian Seminary Professor

How easily the white professor forgets
Heritage represents a high tower
There's no room there for forget-me-nots
Not in these here United States
Not among the 50 states
For we the descendants of slaves remember
We descendants remember
Our forebears were united in common bond
Imagine hands shackled and feet chained
Stripped naked
Black bosoms bare and exposed genitalia
Disembarked at inlets
Shuffled to stockyards and taken stock of
To be made stock of
To be made to work cotton and tobacco fields
Under blazing southern sun
Built barehanded the country's Whitehouse
Forced to serve without liberty
Never allowed to harbor thoughts of freedom
Beaten into thinking as if 3/5th's of a man
Deemed the wildest of beasts
No professor, we forget not our own heritage

No professor, you forget the country's heritage
Tell everybody, "We easily forget"
But we won't
We slave descendants are reminded every day
Your history
It's in the realm of revisionist history
Read that sadistic killer Columbus's journals
Slavery is the African's story
Slavery is the Native American's story
Slavery is the Chinese man's story
Slavery is this country's story
Slavery is the founding father's story
Slavery is your ancestors' story
Something we cannot let you professor
In a moment of absentmindedness
Easily forget
The United States is not only a country
Of immigrants
It's a country of dead slaves
A country of sons and daughters of
Slaves
And we will never easily forget
Our scarlet blue wounds

Stop the Hate!

ONE

Stop the hate.

TWO

Stop the hate.

THREE

Malcom X is quoted as having said,
"If you stick a knife nine inches into my back
and pull it out three inches, that is not
progress.

Even if you pull it all the way out,
that is not progress. Progress is healing
the wound, and America hasn't even begun
to pull out the knife."

FOUR

Stop the hate.

FIVE

Who hates what doesn't look like himself?
Why hate a fully clothed woman? Why hate
the black and brown skin man? Why the
black and brown skin woman, who wears

no makeup, who covers her face, not for
shame, but by religious choice? Is it not The
Beetles who harmonized for the world,

"And when the broken-hearted people /
Living in the world agree / There will be
an answer / Let it be."

SIX

It's called freedom. Every human being's cry
is for freedom. Even Patrick Henry, an American
founding father resoundingly declared,
"Give me liberty or give me death!" How much
more resounding from the immigrant, the
refugee, the undocumented from south of the
border? They too cry freedom.

SEVEN

Stop the hate.

EIGHT

Stop the hate. Say it, speak it, shout it. Shout it
from rooftops! Mark it like a marksman marking
his target; like a sniper, like active shooters: like
someone sniping about an irritant, or some evil.
Hate is an irritant. Hate is evil. Stop the hate. Say
it, speak it, shout it!

Live in loving memoriam Taliesin Myrddin Namkai
and Rick Best, for your selfless sacrifice for the "Muslim,"
for the so-called "other," for the sake of humanity.
No greater love is there than your selfless sacrifices.

Get well soon, Micah Fletcher. I know you, and you
know me O' poet, slam poet. Get well man. Rise!
Declare your muse. Say it, speak it, shout it!

NINE

Before it's too late, stop the hate. The fate of
humanity stands in the wake.

Stop the hate.
Stop the hate.
Stop the hate.

TEN

Say it, speak it, shout it!

Stop the hate!

Revolvers

Whys are fraught with lies

    Why chase them for

Fools never know what belies the lie

    Is this why

Revolutions continue

    From the grasp of revolvers

And to think mankind continues

    To evolve

White Walker

I remember being a gun-toting youngster. Holstered
on my right hip was a silver 6-shooter, reminiscent
of the Roy Rogers and Dale Evans era of the old
west. All the boys in the neighborhood owned
a 6-shooter. Fortunately, it could not shoot real
bullets; even though we pretended it could. It was a
good thing, too, for us youngsters could not afford
the bullets.

Gathering weekday mornings at the usual rallying
point we would pick sides. Shirts and skins
differentiated us. As you can imagine, the shirts
were the good guys and skins bad guys. To be
politically incorrect, shirts were cowboys and the
shirtless them Indians. My soul winces at such
distinction and my shame a lifetime to bear for such
attribution.

Looking back now, I loathed the killers we were
because the Indians always lost the fight, including
arguments afterward as to who had been designated
shot and killed first, often signified by "Pow! I got
you." As if immoral miscreants, we would then
count the number of dead on both sides. Today,
and to my amazement, I have never suffered Post
Traumatic Stress Disorder or PTSD.

Unbeknownst to us, we were being conditioned. Death begins in the imagination, actualized through physical imitation. We youngsters took no thought as to taking our friend's life. What appears so evil and deceptive was the fact our friend(s) would rise to live another day. Just like the White Walkers in the HBO Series Game of Thrones Season 8 Episode 3.

Little did we know we were being groomed to be White Walkers? Imagine that, a little black boy like me a White Walker, killing indiscriminately and without forethought. The miracle—the absence of blood and severed body parts. The permissibility of imagination can be pure evil sometimes, especially in the mind of adolescents, which once was true but no more.

I no longer play with or possess a silver 6-shooter. I own a couple 9mm Glocks with clips holding the standard capacity of 15 rounds. I hardly ever touch them and never run around my neighborhood with friends shooting at them. I am a realist now. Oh, how quickly back then I forgot about my first kill. It was a bird, using a slingshot from my hand.

At the End of the World

I'm not a concept
Nor an anatomy of this argument
A stairwell to the 5th floor
Where there's misunderstanding
However
Whereas a sniper shot his shot
A lift is in the sally port
A sailboat is in need of a sail
So I pump air into the dreaded tire
Acknowledge I'm king on my own
Revel in being autonomous
My mother must know I'm a fairytale
I'm no longer in need of a rook
This princess I found in a pumpkin patch
Her left foot fits my left slipper
On our way to the end of the world
We share a slice of gold cheese
Because some of us have fewer lies to tell
At the end of the world

One America

It has been said,
"There is one America."
One white, one black;
one poor, one rich;
one religious, one secular;
one straight,
the other—
gay;
one gated, one homeless;
one hungry, one fed;
one hopeful, one fearful;
one Conservative,
the other—
Progressive;
and everyone else.
"There is one America"
with scarlet blue wounds.

Andrews Air Force Base 2:33PM

Unfolding terrifying moments. Less enlightening
the unrest a world away. Here, we honor America.
We still honor America. Here, draped in red, white,
and blue, we still honor America. We are sad now:
We the People mourn. Here, we honor America.
We, the red, white, and blue, we mourn. Unfolding
terrifying moments. Less enlightening the world
away. We honor America. Andrews Air Force Base,
2:33pm.

Inauguration Day

the poet has nothing to pen.
however, a poem is needed; not
the poet. as inauguration day
looms, neither comes diction
for the swearing in of the dunce.
syntax must signify the sinner.
saints know this, as do the
angels of the poet's better nature.
displaced is disheveled symbolism.
unwilling to come together is the
country. fake news, unceremoniously
poetic. the poet rues the day.

The 45th President of the United States

He, in this context is a personal pronoun.
He, must not be referenced as a proper noun.
He, will be remembered for being a thief and liar.
He, that womanizer and sexual predator.
He, the egotist, sexist, misogynist, jingoist,
      infatuationist, antagonist, protagonist,
            supremacist, narcissistic, chauvinist...
                  for,

He, is, in this iconic class of dastardly adjectives.
He, in this context is a personal pronoun.

Memorial Day

I.   When I find myself contemplating,
        it's a good feeling sitting under the flag
my father bled red, white, and blue for,

IV.   you know; the glory of our nation. He is not at
        Arlington, but Willamette National Cemetery.
That's good enough for me and my family.

VII.   We were spared the bursting of bombs
        over Baghdad, invasion of Grenada,
and to be sure, the Mekong Delta.

X.   So hot the landing zone, where death sanctioned
        a common will, and courage convened
calculated risk in excursion, leaving to be

XIII.   young men in contemptuous derision
        by men who never served, who were served
in glass houses filled with porcelain

XVI.   made in China and sold in America. Yes,
        do fight the power giving them power,
privilege, and the freedom to subdue.

XIX.   Fools fleece the faculty of common sense
        for selfish arrogance with calls for revolution
as a solution to neocon ideology.

XXII.   The economics of the matter are daunting.
          Palatial is the place wherein I sit. Freedom
        is never more sweet than Memorial Day.

XXV.   When I find myself contemplating,
          it's a good feeling sitting under the flag
        my father bled red, white, and blue for.

Memorial Day 2019

I stand by the wayside
Having never donned the uniform
Taken up arms for battle
Volunteered to serve my country
However, my dad did
And my mother did also
On the home front
To me I have lived free
As the U.S. flag waves freely
My parents are dead now
On the western front
All is quiet, quiet on this
Memorial Day 2019

Touché

Queen Elizabeth II
     cancels Trump meeting.
          The culprit—bone spurs.
Like wild British hounds
     allied nation states howl,
          not at Queen Elizabeth II,
but at Donald J. Trump,
     current president of our
          United States. Donald,
you cowardly escaped having
     to go to Vietnam.
          The culprit—bone spurs.
     Touché
          Queen Elizabeth II,
     Touché

American Abstract

Spring is about quiet and reawakening.

Segregated fields of mustard colored poppies bow
and bow. Most—blurred images.

Pretty pink each stem. Tall and short.

A cream colored sky holds hostage the day. No clouds.

Anchoring the backdrop are jagged edged mountains.
Jim Crow laws will never again rule the day.

Brisk winds the injustice. Inferior border a pale white,
securing its place in the foreground.

If only this abstract could speak.

Before Dawn

He/she fell asleep after the engine started
It happened as evening ended and sunrise arose
This truth I know—things have passed
For others—things will begin
Of course, at this moment, he/she's dreaming
When either one awakes he/she will be
As old and as new as ever
As will their scarlet blue wounds

God Portend

Unworthy Mr. President.
Having set myself to write to you,
god portend shame upon you who's
taken to herself your name.

With trained eyes, pretty pennies
are never spurned, words of poetry
kept sparse, never to come a
fake surmise.

Can you discern vitriol in
this my musing? If only you could
comprehend what I've said, sir.
Only you. If only you could, sir.

For the Record Please

In May, there have been questions
Mostly on television and in newspapers
Before Senate subcommittees and review boards
Where men and women swear an oath to be truthful
Knowing they will lie when the need arises
Even though having sworn an oath
Before God and fellow man
On a Bible where lifted is their other hand
Under the tree of liberty and justice
Christian ethic, "Thou shall not lie"
The concept of having "misspoke" is promulgated
Seared conscience is not a medical diagnosis
Mr. I Can't Recall senator is the new moniker

For the record, please speak louder, sir
Please, speak louder
Please, speak louder, sir!
We can't hear you! Speak louder for the record
Thank you

In June there will be more questions
Not on television or in newspapers
Not before Senate subcommittees and review boards
Where men and women swore an oath to be truthful
Even though having sworn an oath
Before God and fellow man
On a Bible where lifted is their other hand

Under the tree of liberty and justice
Christian ethic, "Thou shall not lie"
For every one of them will have gone home
Carrying their conscience in the recess of their mind
Knowing to some small degree they misled
The American people who need them to govern
Not investigate or to castigate
But to simply tell the truth

Send this Reply

Pacifists see pragmatists
as delusional.
Violence perpetuates violence.
Predators seek prey.
A pod of killer whales
attack in frenzy.
Humpback whales
defend gray whales.
So much for detente.
Send this reply.
Pacifists are not women
or madmen, just future subjects,
servants of despots,
oligarchs, and madness.

Americana

there is no market for me
other than illiteracy
i write what blacks won't buy
i create what whites won't read
sadly, others are unaware of me
thus, the state of my poetry finds
there is no market for me
therefore, my sense of Americana
my shelf-life, myself, my very life
in terms of poetic residency
there's no market for me
other than illiteracy

Animals

Animals thin,
Animals wide,
Animals that laugh,
Animals that cry,
Animals that meow,
Animals that moo,
I like animals,
I hope you do too!

Remi Massey is a second grade student attending
school in Oregon.

CPSIA information can be obtained
at www.ICGtesting.com
Printed in the USA
FSHW010754091219
64692FS